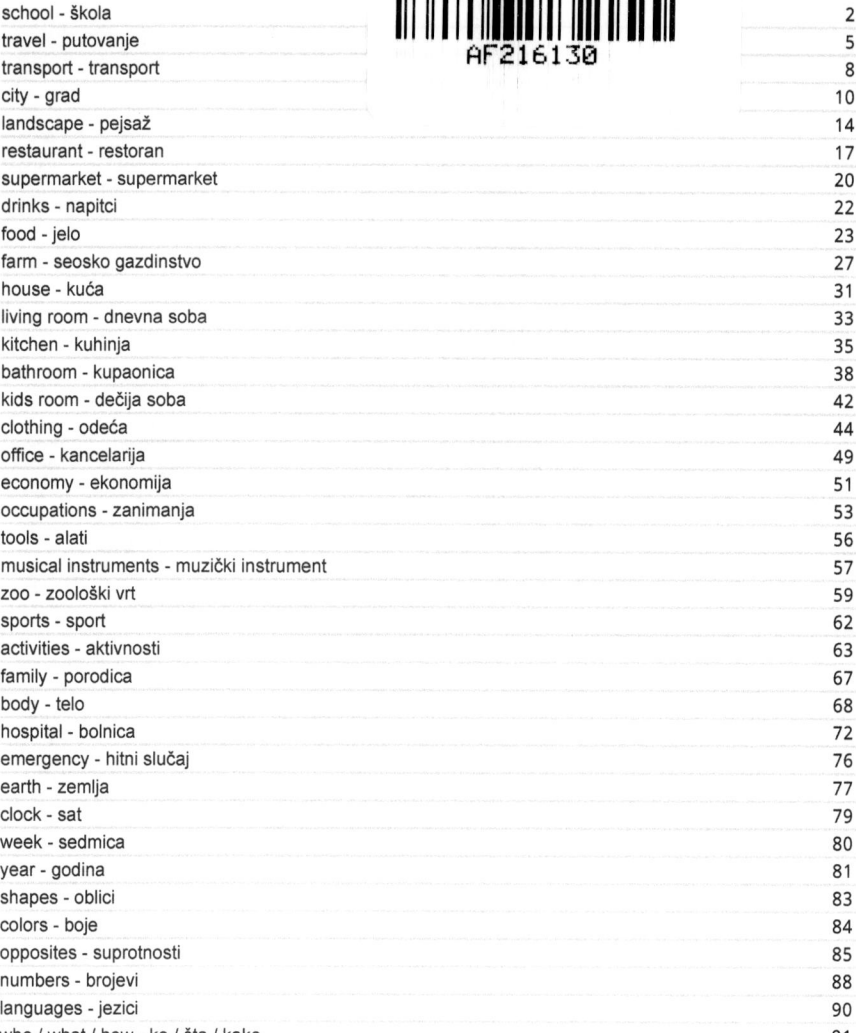

school - škola	2
travel - putovanje	5
transport - transport	8
city - grad	10
landscape - pejsaž	14
restaurant - restoran	17
supermarket - supermarket	20
drinks - napitci	22
food - jelo	23
farm - seosko gazdinstvo	27
house - kuća	31
living room - dnevna soba	33
kitchen - kuhinja	35
bathroom - kupaonica	38
kids room - dečija soba	42
clothing - odeća	44
office - kancelarija	49
economy - ekonomija	51
occupations - zanimanja	53
tools - alati	56
musical instruments - muzički instrument	57
zoo - zoološki vrt	59
sports - sport	62
activities - aktivnosti	63
family - porodica	67
body - telo	68
hospital - bolnica	72
emergency - hitni slučaj	76
earth - zemlja	77
clock - sat	79
week - sedmica	80
year - godina	81
shapes - oblici	83
colors - boje	84
opposites - suprotnosti	85
numbers - brojevi	88
languages - jezici	90
who / what / how - ko / šta / kako	91
where - gde	92

Impressum
Verlag: BABADADA GmbH, Nedderfeld 112 , 22529 Hamburg
Geschäftsführer / Verlagsleitung: Harald Hof
Druck: Books on Demand GmbH, In de Tarpen 42, 22848 Norderstedt

Imprint
Publisher: BABADADA GmbH, Nedderfeld 112 , 22529 Hamburg, Germany
Managing Director / Publishing direction: Harald Hof
Print: Books on Demand GmbH, In de Tarpen 42, 22848 Norderstedt

school
škola

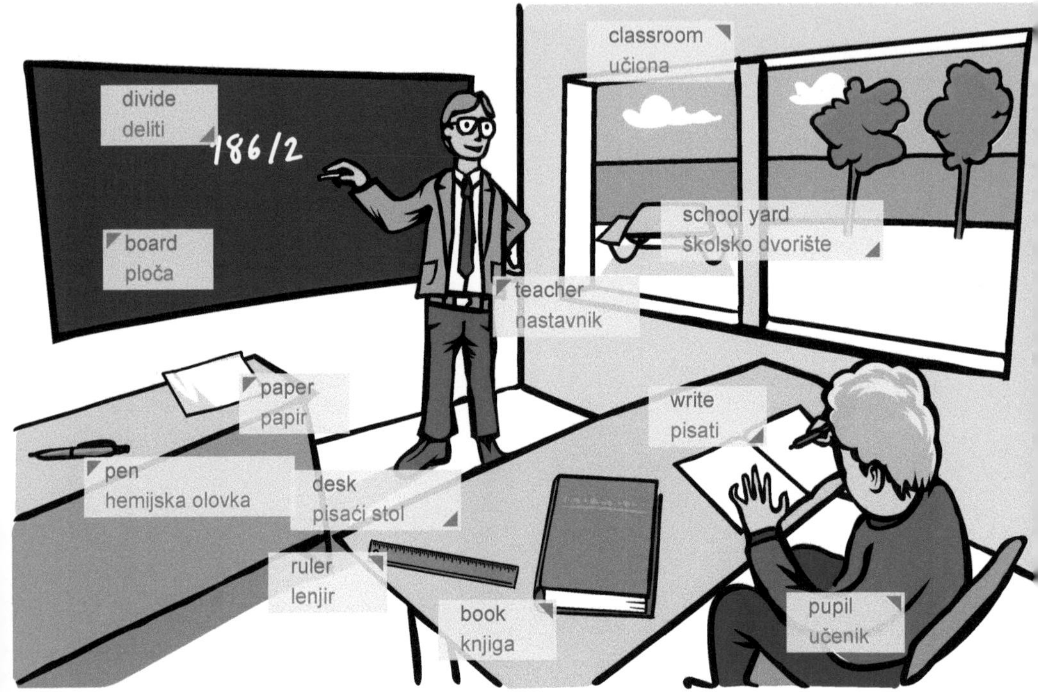
classroom
učiona
divide
deliti
186/2
board
ploča
school yard
školsko dvorište
teacher
nastavnik
paper
papir
write
pisati
pen
hemijska olovka
desk
pisaći stol
ruler
lenjir
book
knjiga
pupil
učenik

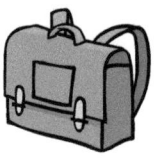

satchel
torba

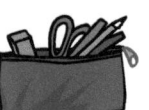

pencil case
pernica

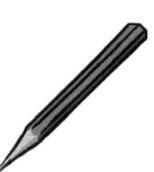

pencil
grafitna olovka

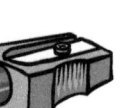

pencil sharpener
šiljilo za olovke

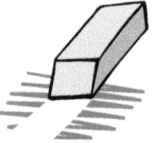

rubber
gumica za brisanje

drawing pad
blok za crtanje

drawing
crtež

paintbrush
kist

paint box
kutija sa bojama

scissors
makaze

glue
lepilo

exercise book
beležnica

homework
domaći zadatak

number
broj

2+2

add
sabirati

subtract
oduzimati

multiply
množiti

calculate
računati

A

letter
slovo

ABCDEFG
HIJKLMN
OPQRSTU
VWXYZ

alphabet
abeceda

word
reč

text
tekst

read
čitati

chalk
kreda

lesson
čas

register
dnevnik

examination
ispit

certificate
svedočanstvo

school uniform
školska uniforma

education
obrazovanje

encyclopedia
leksikon

university
univerzitet

microscope
mikroskop

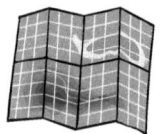

map
karta

waste-paper basket
košara za papir

travel
putovanje

hotel
hotel
Grand
hostel
prenoćište
ROOMS
currency exchange office
menjačnica
EXCHANGE
car
auto

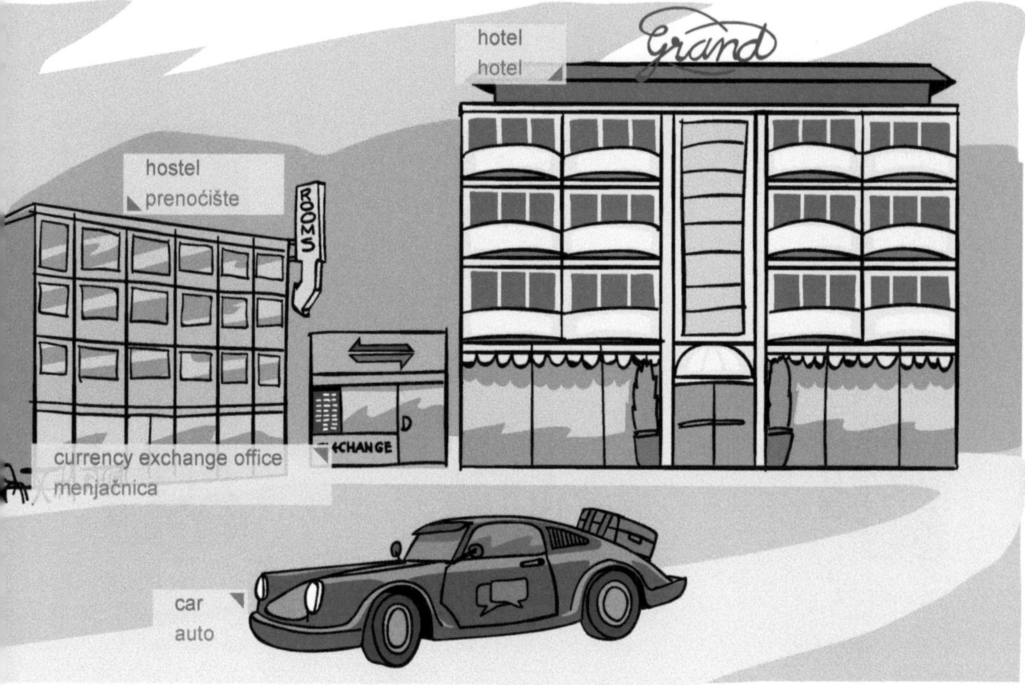

language
jezik

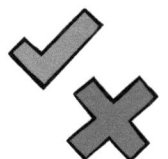

yes / no
da / ne

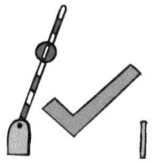

Okay
okej

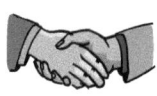

hello
zdravo

translator
prevodilac

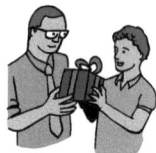

Thank you
hvala

how much is...?

Koliko košta...?

I don´t get it

ne razumem

problem

problem

Good evening!

dobro veče!

Good morning!

Dobro jutro!

Good night!

Laku noć!

goodbye

doviđenja

direction

smer

luggage

prtljaga

bag

torba

backpack

ruksak

guest

gost

room

soba

sleeping bag

vreća za spavanje

tent

šator

tourist information

turističke informacije

beach

plaža

credit card

kreditna kartica

breakfast

doručak

lunch

ručak

dinner

večera

Ticket

karta za vožnju

elevator

lift

stamp

poštanska markica

border

granica

customs

carina

embassy

ambasada

visa

viza

passport

pasoš

transport
transport

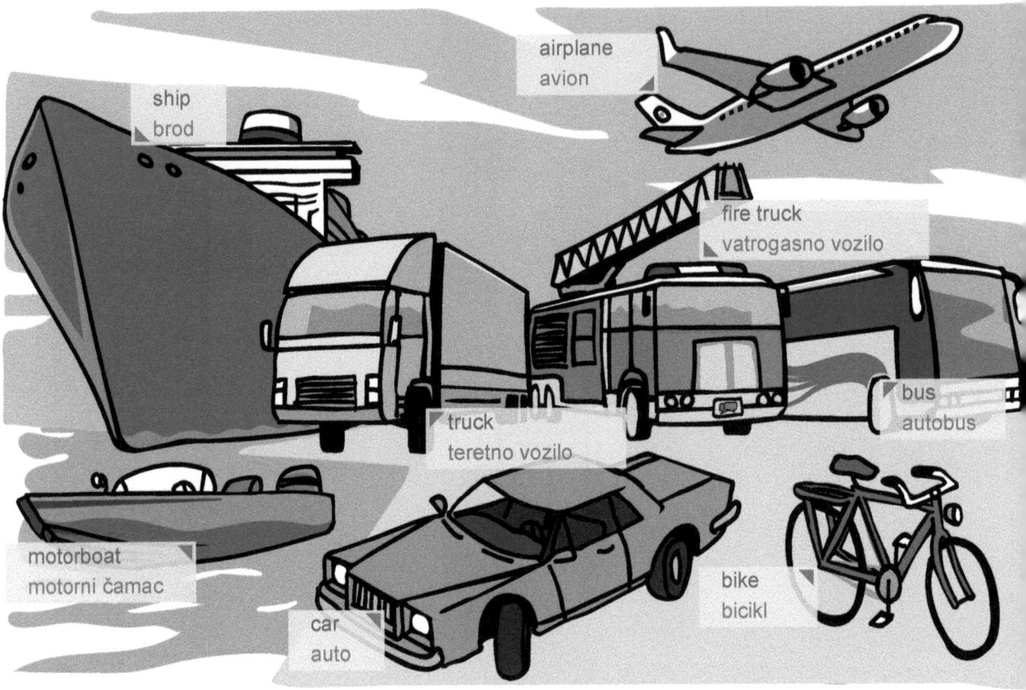

ship
brod
airplane
avion
fire truck
vatrogasno vozilo
bus
autobus
truck
teretno vozilo
motorboat
motorni čamac
car
auto
bike
bicikl

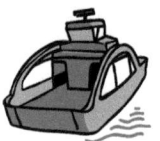

ferry

trajekt

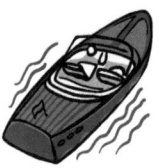

boat

čamac

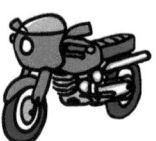

motorbike

motocikl

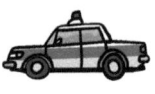

police car

policijski auto

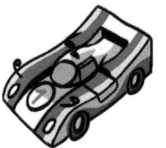

racing car

trkaći auto

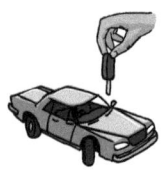

rental car

iznajmljeno auto

car sharing

delenje automobila

tow truck

vučno vozilo

garbage truck

vozilo za odvoz smeća

engine

motor

fuel

benzin

fuel station

benzinska stanica

traffic sign

saobraćajni znak

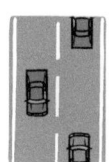

traffic

saobraćaj

traffic jam

zastoj

parking lot

parkiralište

train station

železnička stanica

tracks

šine

train

voz

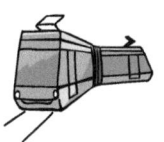

tram

tramvaj

wagon

vagon

helicopter

helikopter

airport

aerodrom

tower

kula

passenger

putnik

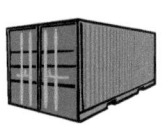

container

kontejner

carton

karton

cart

kolica

basket

korpa

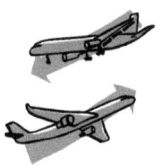

take off / land

uzleteti / sleteti

city

grad

village

selo

city center

centar grada

house

kuća

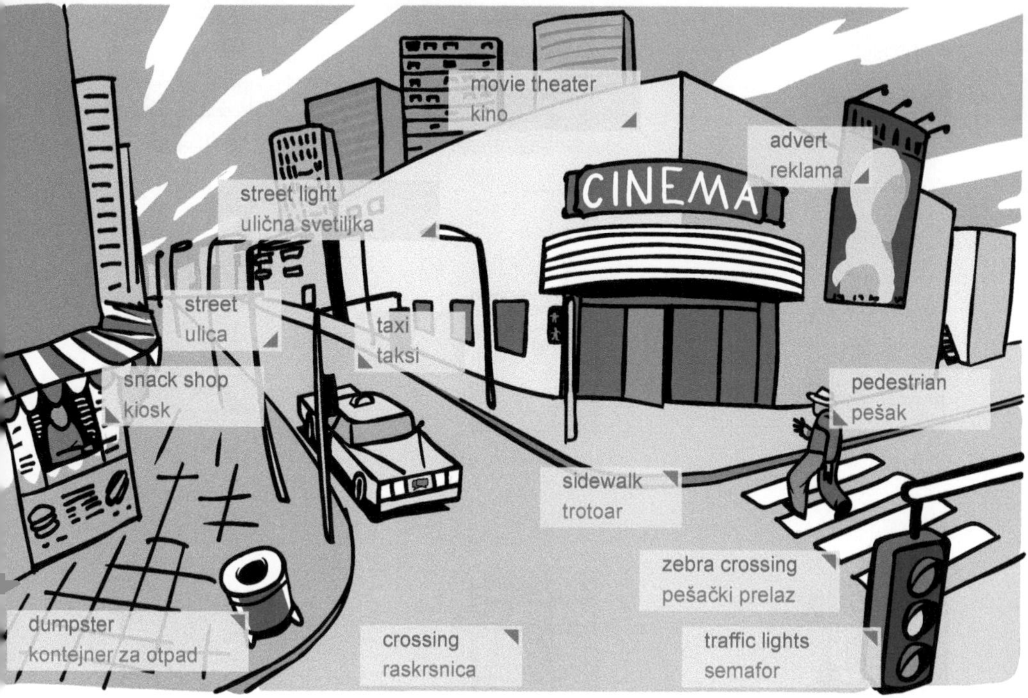

movie theater
kino

advert
reklama

street light
ulična svetiljka

CINEMA

street
ulica

taxi
taksi

snack shop
kiosk

pedestrian
pešak

sidewalk
trotoar

zebra crossing
pešački prelaz

dumpster
kontejner za otpad

crossing
raskrsnica

traffic lights
semafor

hut
koliba

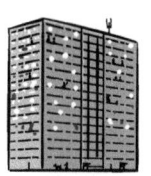

apartment
stan

train station
železnička stanica

city hall
većnica

museum
muzej

school
škola

university

univerzitet

bank

banka

hospital

bolnica

hotel

hotel

pharmacy

apoteka

office

kancelarija

book shop

knjižara

shop

prodavnica

flower shop

cvećara

supermarket

supermarket

market

trg

department store

robna kuća

fishmonger's shop

ribarnica

mall

trgovački centar

harbor

luka

park

park

bench

klupa

bridge

most

stairs

stepenice

subway

podzemna železnica

tunnel

tunel

bus stop

autobuska stanica

bar

bar

restaurant

restoran

postbox

poštansko sanduče

street sign

ulični znak

parking meter

parkirni automat

zoo

zoološki vrt

swimming pool

bazen

mosque

džamija

farm

seosko gazdinstvo

pollution

zagađenje okoline

cemetery

groblje

church

crkva

playground

igralište

temple

hram

landscape
pejsaž

signpost
putokaz

path
put

meadow
livada

stone
kamen

tree
drvo

hiker
šetač

river
reka

grass
trava

flower
cvijet

valley

dolina

hill

planina

lake

jezero

forest

šuma

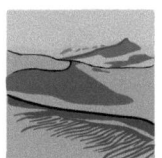

desert

pustinja

volcano

vulkan

castle

dvorac

rainbow

duga

mushroom

gljiva

palm tree

palma

mosquito

moskito

fly

muva

ant

mrav

bee

pčela

spider

pauk

beetle

buba

frog

žaba

squirrel

veverica

hedgehog

jež

hare

zec

owl

sova

bird

ptica

swan

labud

boar

divlja svinja

deer

jelen

moose

los

dam

nasip

wind turbine

vetrenjača

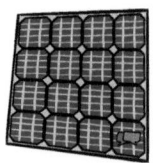

solar panel

solarna ploča

climate

klima

restaurant
restoran

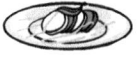

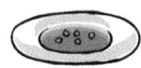

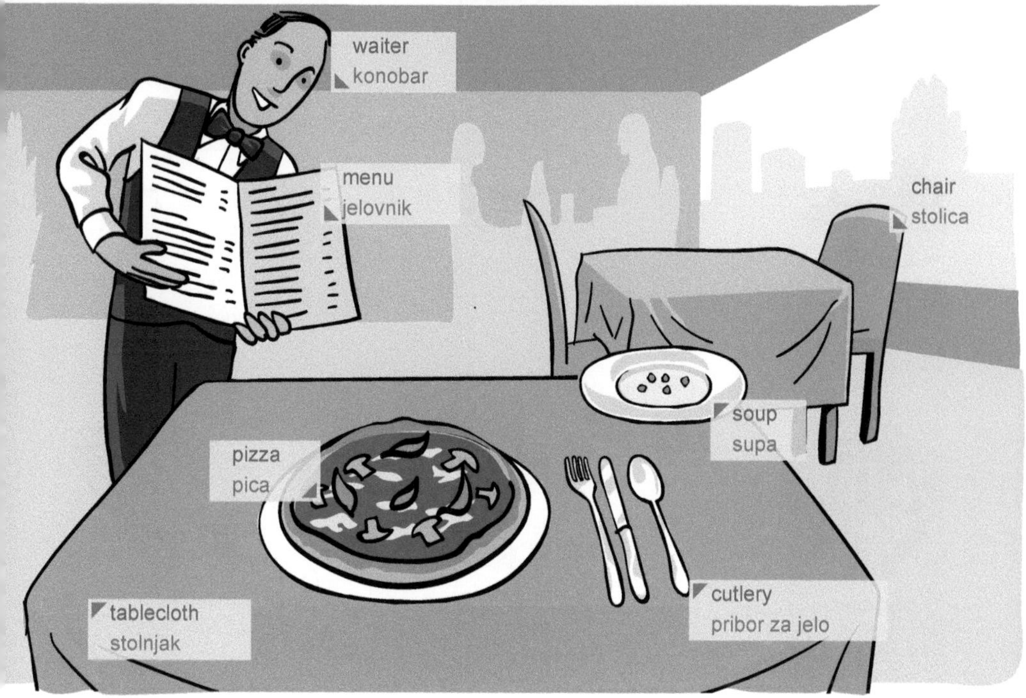
waiter
konobar
menu
jelovnik
chair
stolica
soup
supa
pizza
pica
cutlery
pribor za jelo
tablecloth
stolnjak

starter

predjelo

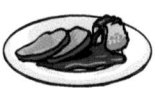

main course

glavno jelo

dessert

desert

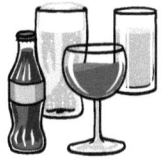

drinks

napitci

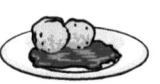

food

jelo

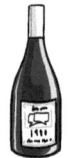

bottle

flaša

fast food

brza hrana

street food

imbis hrana

teapot

čajnik

sugar bowl

doza za šećer

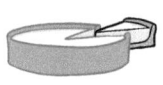

portion

porcija

espresso machine

aparat za espresso

high chair

visoka stolica

bill

račun

tray

poslužavnik

knife

nož

fork

viljuška

spoon

kašika

teaspoon

čajna kašika

serviette

salveta

glass

čaša

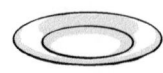

plate

tanjir

soup plate

tanjir za supu

saucer

tanjirić

sauce

sos

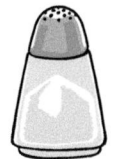

salt shaker

soljenka

pepper mill

mlin za biber

vinegar

sirće

oil

ulje

spices

začini

ketchup

kečap

mustard

senf

mayonnaise

majoneza

supermarket

supermarket

special offer
ponuda
FOR
customer
kupac
dairy products
mlečni proizvodi
fruit
voće
shopping cart
kolica za kupovinu

BUTCHERS

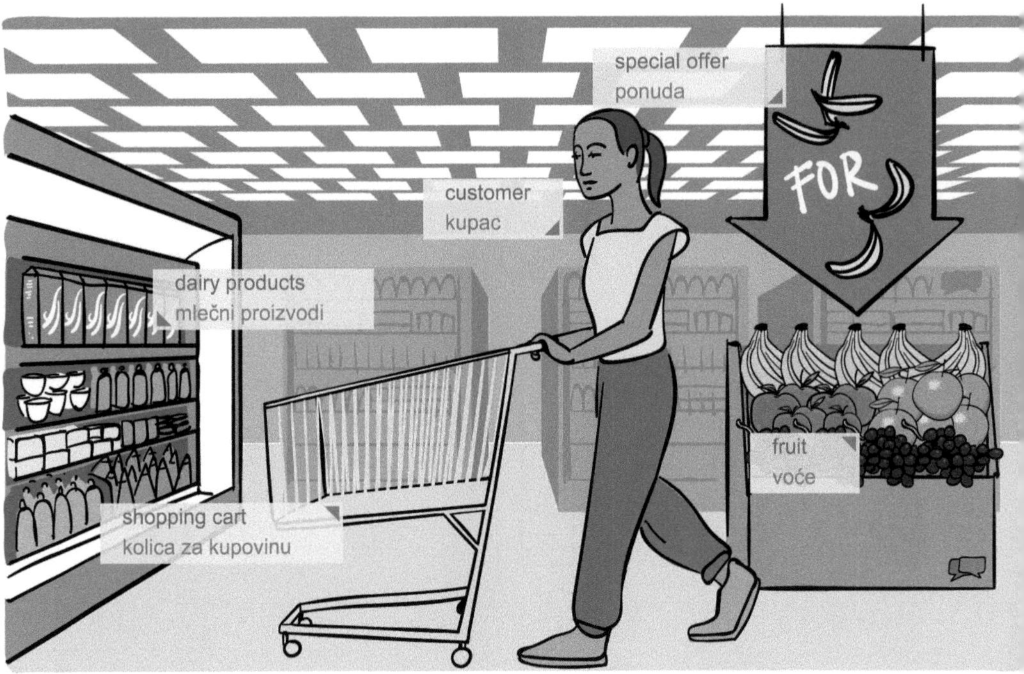

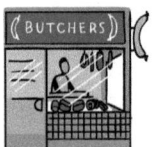

butcher's shop

mesnica

BAKERY

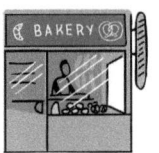

bakery

pekara

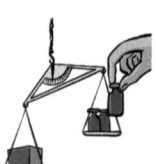

weigh

vagati

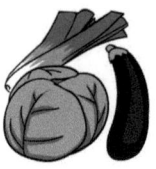

vegetables

povrće

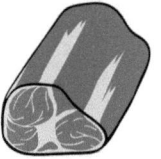

meat

meso

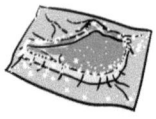

frozen food

smrznuta hrana

cold cuts
narezak

canned food
konzerve

detergent
sredstvo za pranje

candy
slatkiši

household products
artikli za domaćinstvo

cleaning products
sredstva za čišćenje

sales representative
prodavačica

cash register
blagajna

cashier
blagajnik

shopping list
lista za kupovinu

opening hours
vreme rada

wallet
novčanik

credit card
kreditna kartica

bag
torba

plastic bag
plastična kesa

water

voda

juice

sok

milk

mleko

coke

kola

wine

vino

beer

pivo

alcohol

alkohol

cocoa

kakao

tea

čaj

coffee

kava

espresso

espresso

cappuccino

cappuccino

banana

banana

apple

jabuka

orange

narandža

melon

lubenica

lemon

limun

carrot

šargarepa

garlic

beli luk

bamboo

bambus

onion

luk

mushroom

gljiva

nuts

orašasti plodovi

noodles

rezanci

spaghetti

špagete

rice

riža

salad

salata

fries

pomfrit

fried potatoes

pečeni krumpir

pizza

pica

hamburger

hamburger

sandwich

sendvič

escalope

šnicla

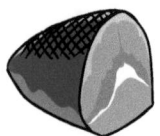

ham

šunka

salami

salama

sausage

kobasica

chicken

kokoš

roast

pečenje

fish

riba

porridge oats

zobene pahuljice

muesli

musli

cornflakes

kukuruzne pahuljice

flour

brašno

croissant

kroasan

bread roll

pecivo

bread

hleb

toast

toast

cookies

keksi

butter

maslac

curd

sveži sir

cake

kolač

egg

jaje

fried egg

jaje na oko

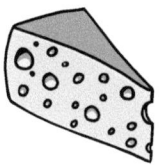

cheese

sir

food - jelo

ice cream

sladoled

sugar

šećer

honey

med

jelly

marmelada

nougat cream

nugat krema

curry

kari

goat	cow	calf
koza	krava	tele

pig	piglet	bull
svinja	prase	bik

goose

guska

duck

patka

chick

pilići

hen

kokoš

cockerel

petao

rat

pacov

cat

mačka

mouse

miš

ox

vol

dog

pas

dog house

kućica za psa

garden hose

vrtno crevo

watering can

kanta za polivanje

scythe

kosa

plow

plug

farm - seosko gazdinstvo

sickle

srp

hoe

motika

pitchfork

viljuška za đubrivo

axe

sekira

pushcart

tačke

trough

korito

milk can

posuda za mleko

sack

vreća

fence

ograda

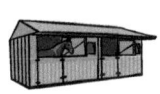

stable

štala

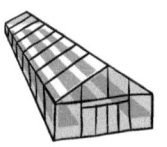

greenhouse

staklenik

soil

zemlja

seed

seme

fertilizer

đubrivo

combine harvester

kombajn

harvest

žeti

harvest

žetva

yams

jams začin

wheat

pšenica

soya

soja

potato

krumpir

corn

kukuruz

rapeseed

uljana repica

fruit tree

voćka

manioc

gomolj manioke

grain

žitarice

house
kuća

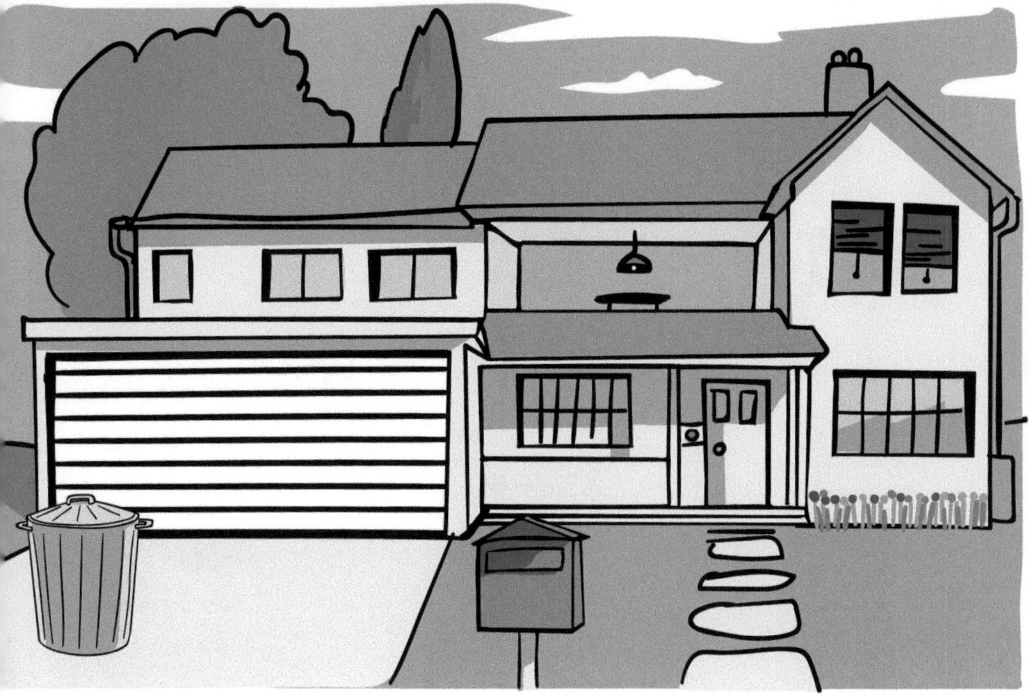

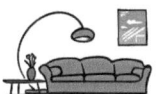

living room

dnevna soba

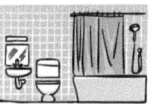

bathroom

kupaonica

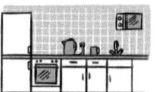

kitchen

kuhinja

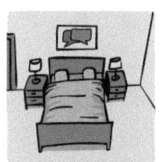

bedroom

spavaća soba

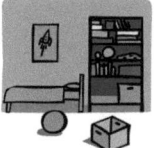

kids room

dečija soba

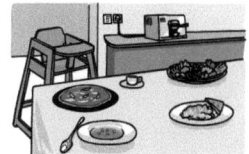

dining room

trpezarija

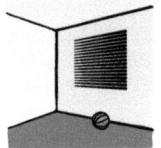

floor

pod

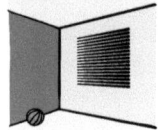

wall

zid

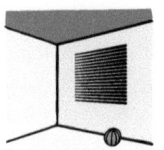

ceiling

strop

cellar

podrum

sauna

sauna

balcony

balkon

terrace

terasa

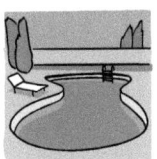

pool

bazen

lawn mower

kosilica za travu

sheet

posteljina za krevet

bedspread

deka za krevet

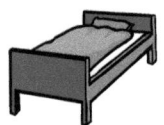

bed

krevet

broom

metla

bucket

kanta

switch

prekidač

living room
dnevna soba

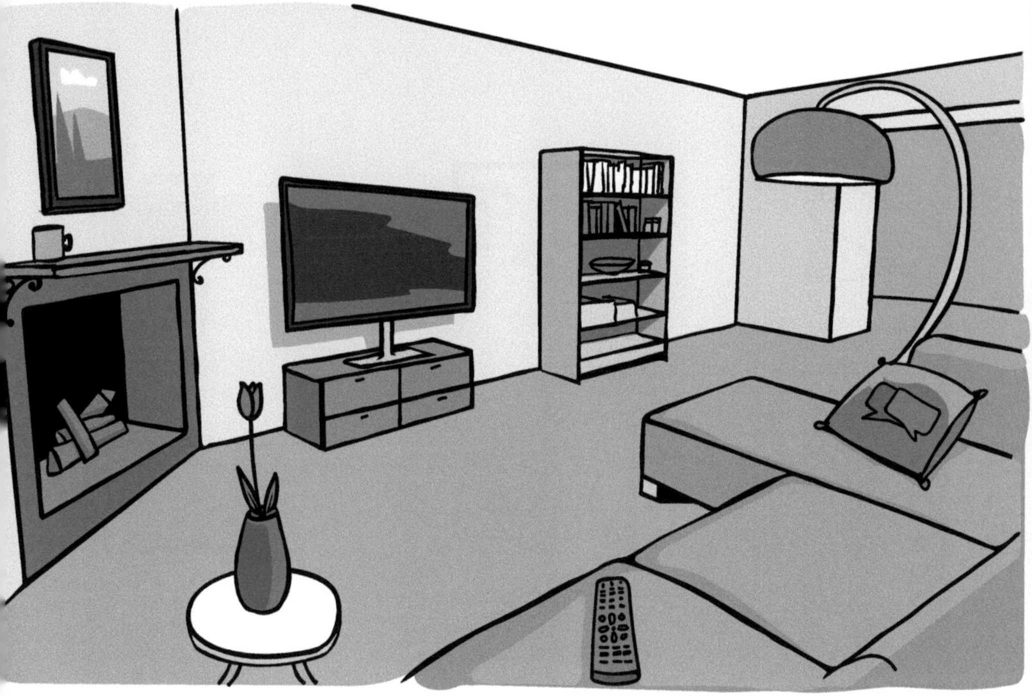

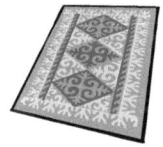

carpet

tepih

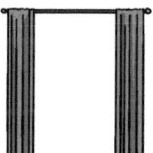

drape

zavesa

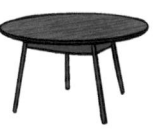

table

sto

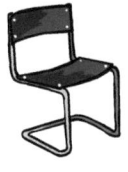

chair

stolica

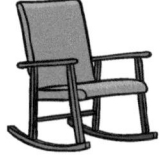

rocking chair

stolica za njihanje

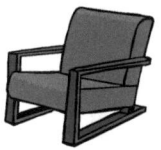

armchair

fotelja

book

knjiga

blanket

deka

decoration

dekoracija

firewood

drvo za ogrev

film

film

stereo system

hi-fi uređaj

key

ključ

newspaper

novine

painting

slika na platnu

poster

poster

radio

radio

notebook

blok za pisanje

vacuum cleaner

usisivač

cactus

kaktus

candle

sveća

kitchen
kuhinja

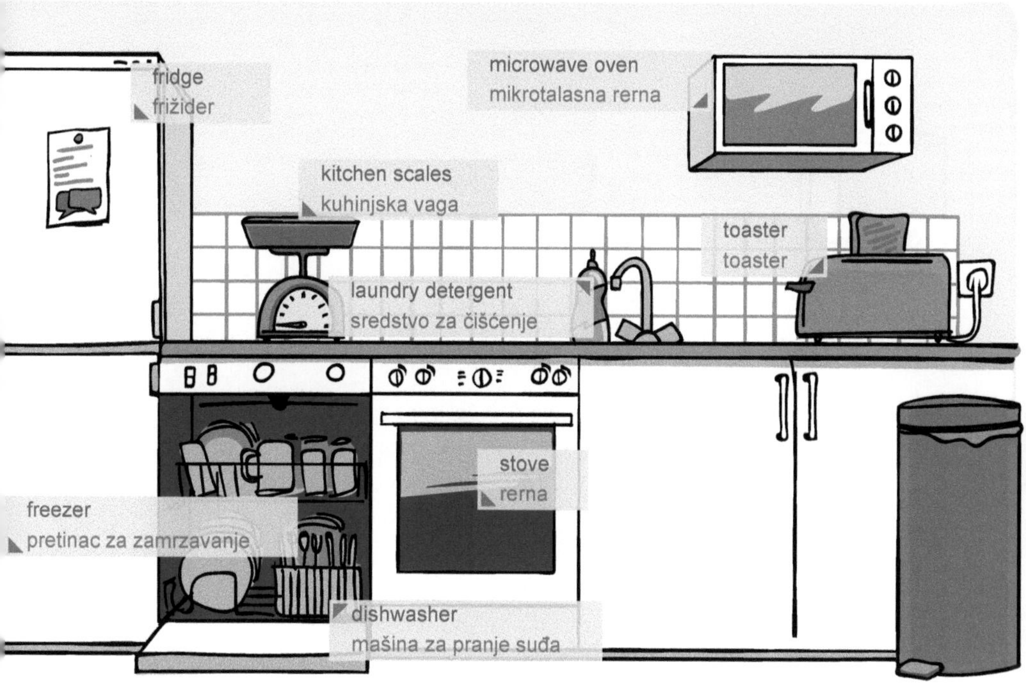

fridge
frižider
microwave oven
mikrotalasna rerna
kitchen scales
kuhinjska vaga
toaster
toaster
laundry detergent
sredstvo za čišćenje
stove
rerna
freezer
pretinac za zamrzavanje
dishwasher
mašina za pranje suđa

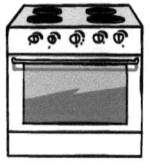

cooker
šporet

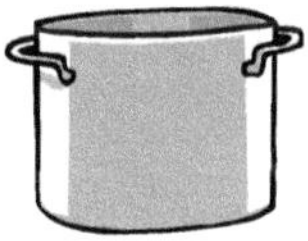
pot
lonac

cast-iron pot
gvozdeni lonac

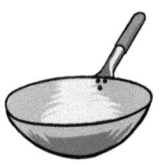

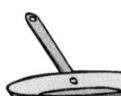

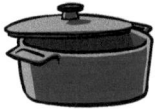

wok / kadai
wok / kadai

pan
tava

kettle
kuvalo za vodu

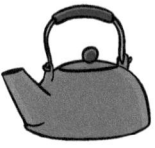

steamer

kuvalo na paru

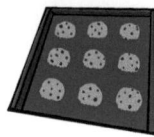

baking tray

lim za pečenje

crockery

posuđe

mug

čaša

bowl

posuda

chopsticks

štapići za jelo

ladle

kutlača

spatula

lopatica

whisk

penjača

strainer

sito za kuvanje

sieve

sito

grater

ribež

mortar

mužar

barbecue

roštilj

fireplace

ognjište

kitchen - kuhinja

chopping board

daska

rolling pin

oklagija

corkscrew

vadičep

can

konzerva

can opener

otvarač konzervi

oven cloth

krpa za lonac

sink

sudoper

brush

četka

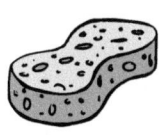

sponge

sunđer

blender

mikser

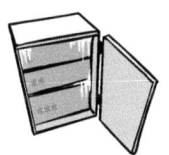

deep freezer

zamrzivač

baby bottle

flašica za bebe

tap

slavina za vodu

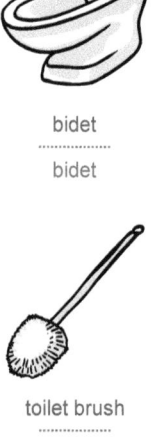

bathroom
kupaonica

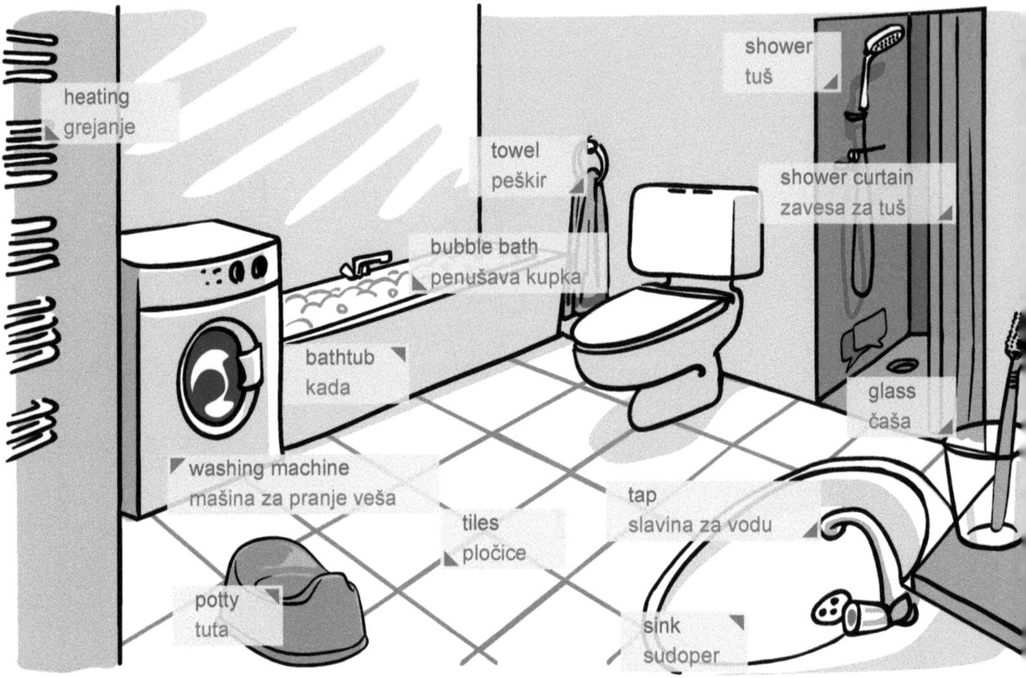
heating
grejanje
towel
peškir
shower
tuš
shower curtain
zavesa za tuš
bubble bath
penušava kupka
bathtub
kada
glass
čaša
washing machine
mašina za pranje veša
tap
slavina za vodu
tiles
pločice
potty
tuta
sink
sudoper

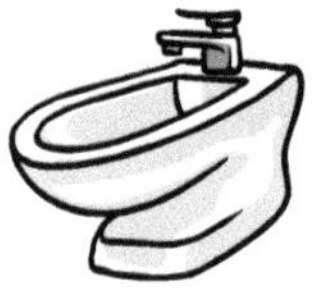

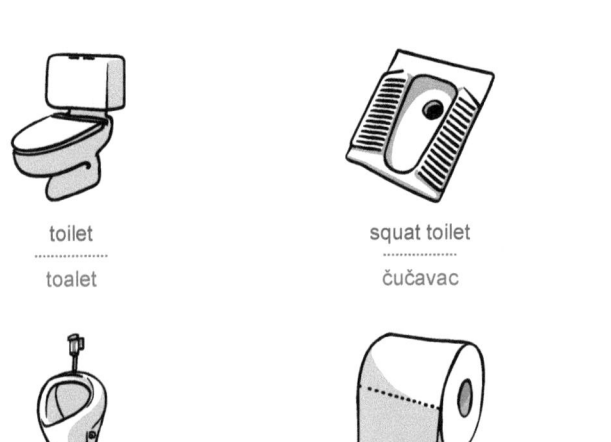

toilet

toalet

squat toilet

čučavac

bidet

bidet

urinal

pisoar

toilet paper

toaletni papir

toilet brush

četka za toalet

toothbrush

četkica za zube

toothpaste

pasta za zube

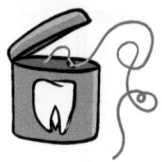

dental floss

konac za zube

wash

prati

hand shower

tuš ručica

douche

tuš za pranje intimnih delova

basin

lavor

back brush

četka za pranje leđa

soap

sapun

shower gel

gel za tuširanje

shampoo

šampon

flannel

krpa za pranje

drain

odvod

creme

krema

deodorant

dezodorans

mirror

ogledalo

hand mirror

kozmetičko ogledalo

razor

brijač

shaving foam

pena za brijanje

aftershave

losion za posle brijanja

comb

češalj

brush

četka

hair-dryer

fen za kosu

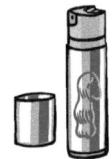

hairspray

sprej za kosu

makeup

makeup

lipstick

ruž za usne

nail varnish

lak za nokte

cotton wool

vata

nail scissors

makaze za nokte

perfume

parfem

washbag

kozmetička torbica

stool

stolica

weighing scales

vaga

bathrobe

ogrtač

rubber gloves

rukavice za čišćenje

tampon

tampon

sanitary towel

uložak

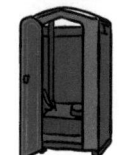

chemical toilet

hemijski toalet

kids room

dečija soba

alarm clock
budilnik
cuddly toy
plišana igračka
toy car
auto igračka
rattle
zvečka
doll's house
kućica za lutke
present
poklon

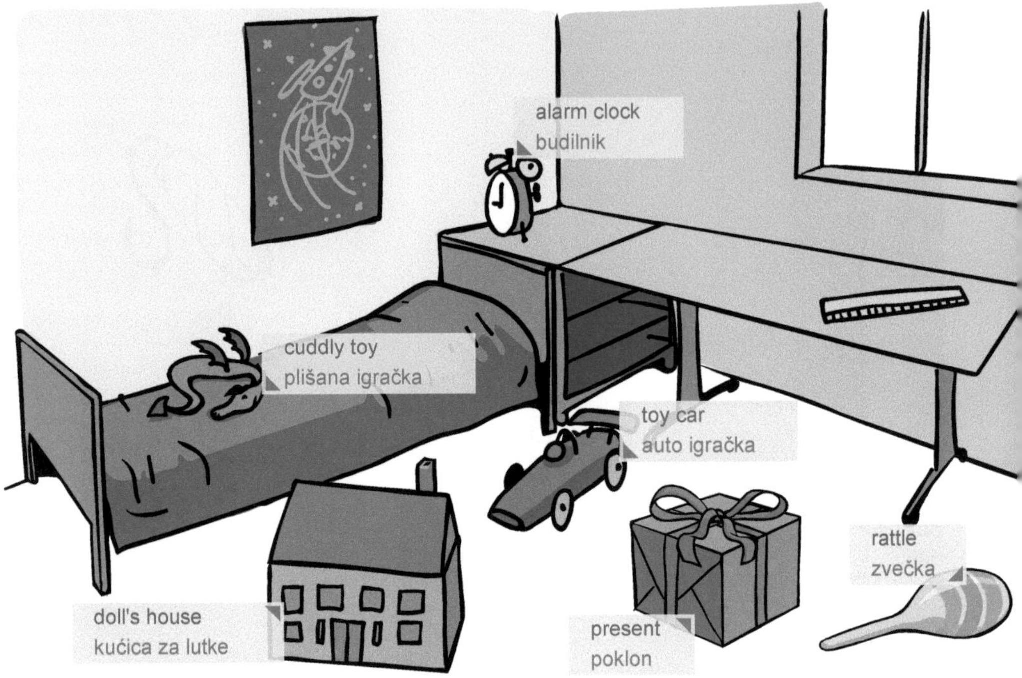

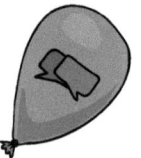

balloon

balon

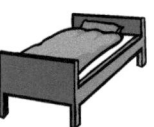

bed

krevet

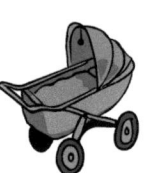

stroller

dječija kolica

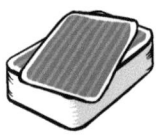

deck of cards

igra s kartama

jigsaw

slagalica

SUPER
MEGA

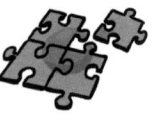

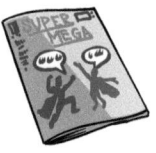

comic

strip

lego bricks

lego kockice

toy blocks

kockice za slaganje

action figure

akcioni junak

romper suit

benkica za bebe

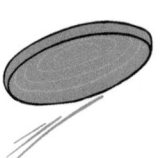

frisbee

frizbi

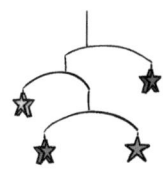

mobile

viseće igračke

board game

društvene igre

dice

kocka

model train set

minijaturna željeznica

pacifier

duda

party

zabava

picture book

slikovnica

ball

lopta

doll

lutka

play

igrati

sandpit

pješčanik

swing

ljuljačka

toys

igračka

video game console

konzola za igre

tricycle

tricikl

teddy bear

tedi

wardrobe

ormar

clothing

odeća

socks

kratke čarape

stockings

čarape

tights

hulahopke

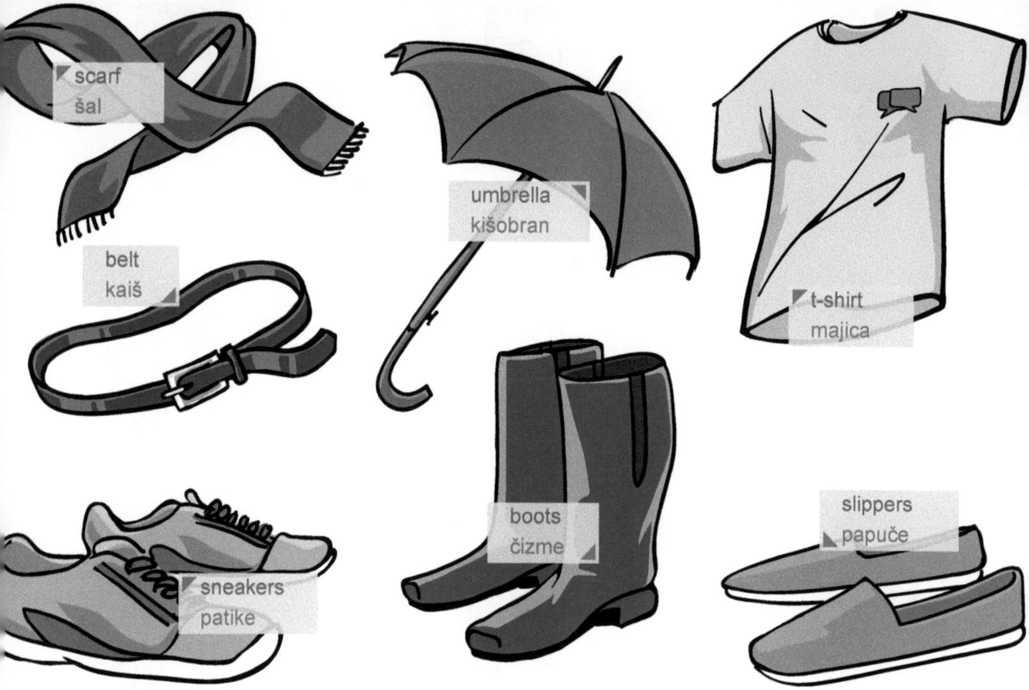

scarf
šal

umbrella
kišobran

t-shirt
majica

belt
kaiš

boots
čizme

slippers
papuče

sneakers
patike

sandals	shoes	rubber boots
sandale	cipele	gumene čizme

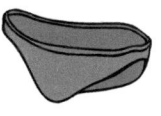  

underwear	bra	undershirt
gaćice	grudnjak	potkošulja

body

bodi

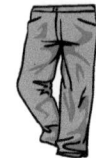

pants

pantalone

jeans

farmerke

skirt

suknja

blouse

bluza

shirt

košulja

pullover

džemper

sweater

džemper s kapuljačom

blazer

sako

jacket

jakna

coat

kaput

raincoat

kabanica

costume

kostim

dress

haljina

wedding dress

venčanica

suit

odelo

nightgown

spavaćica

pajamas

pidžama

sari

sari

headscarf

marama za glavu

turban

turban

burka

burka

kaftan

kaftan

abaya

abaja

swimsuit

kupaći kostim

trunks

kupaće gaćice

shorts

kratke pantalone

tracksuit

odeća za trening

apron

kecelja

gloves

rukavice

button

dugme

glasses

naočare

bracelet

narukvica

necklace

ogrlica

ring

prsten

earring

naušnica

cap

kapa

coat hanger

vešalica

hat

šešir

tie

kravata

zip

patent zatvarač

helmet

kaciga

braces

naramenice

school uniform

školska uniforma

uniform

uniforma

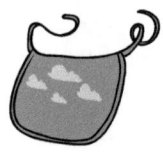

bib

podbradak

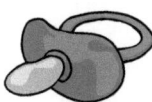

pacifier

duda

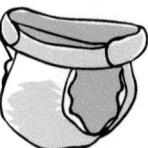

diaper

pelena

office
kancelarija

server
server
filing cabinet
ormar za spise
printer
štampač
paper
papir
monitor
monitor
mouse
miš
desk
pisaći stol
folder
mapa
keyboard
tastatura
waste-paper basket
košara za papir
computer
kompjuter
chair
stolica

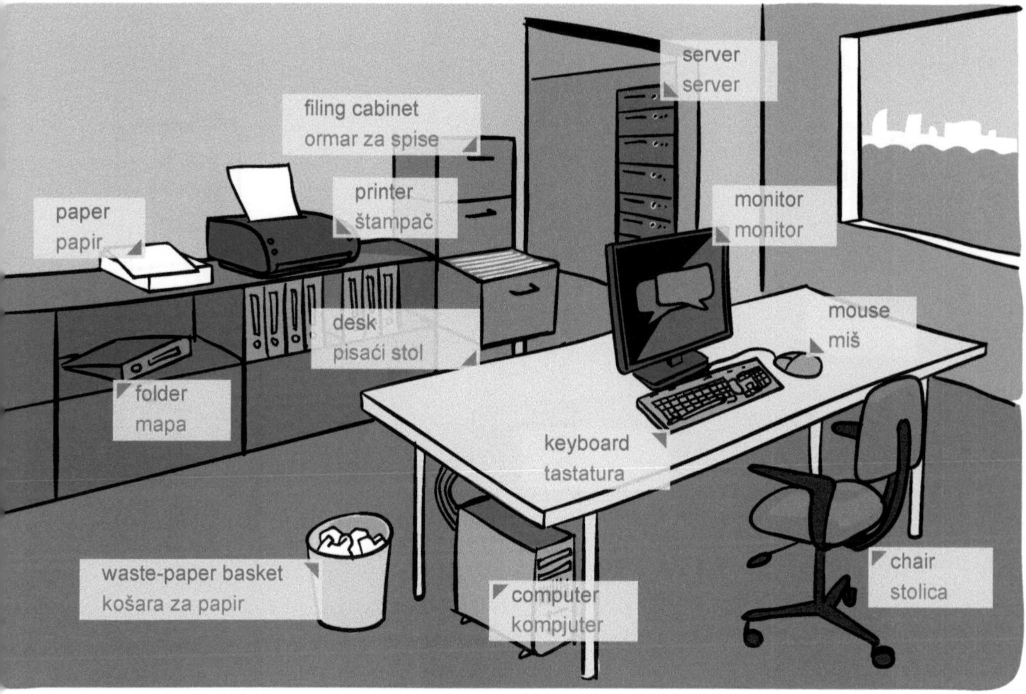

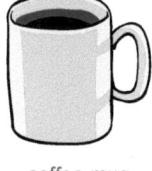

coffee mug

šalica za kavu

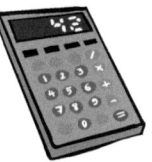

calculator

kalkulator

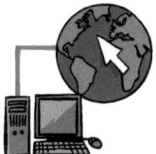

internet

internet

laptop

laptop

letter

pismo

message

poruka

cell phone

mobilni telefon

network

mreža

photocopier

uređaj za kopiranje

software

softver

telephone

telefon

plug socket

utičnica

fax machine

faks

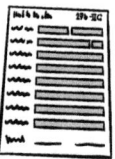

form

formular

document

dokument

buy

kupovati

pay

platiti

trade

trgovati

money

novac

dollar

dolar

euro

evro

yen

jen

rouble

rublja

Swiss franc

švajcarski franak

renminbi yuan

renmindbi juan

rupee

rupija

cash point

automat za novac

currency exchange office

menjačnica

gold

zlato

silver

srebro

oil

nafta

energy

energija

price

cena

contract

ugovor

tax

porez

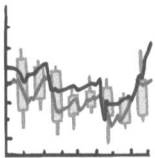

stock

deonica

work

raditi

employee

službenik

employer

poslodavac

factory

fabrika

shop

prodavnica

police officer
policajac

fireman
vatrogasac

cook
kuvar

doctor
lekar

pilot
pilot

gardener

vrtlar

carpenter

stolar

seamstress

krojačica

judge

sudija

chemist

hemičar

actor

glumac

bus driver

vozač autobusa

taxi driver

vozač taksija

fisherman

ribar

cleaning lady

čistačica

roofer

krovopokrivač

waiter

konobar

hunter

lovac

painter

slikar

baker

pekar

electrician

električar

builder

građevinski radnik

engineer

inženjer

butcher

mesar

plumber

limar

postman

poštar

soldier

vojnik

architect

arhitekta

cashier

blagajnik

florist

cvećar

hairdresser

frizer

conductor

kondukter

mechanic

mehaničar

captain

kapetan

dentist

zubar

scientist

naučnik

rabbi

rabi

imam

imam

monk

monah

pastor

svećenik

tools
alati

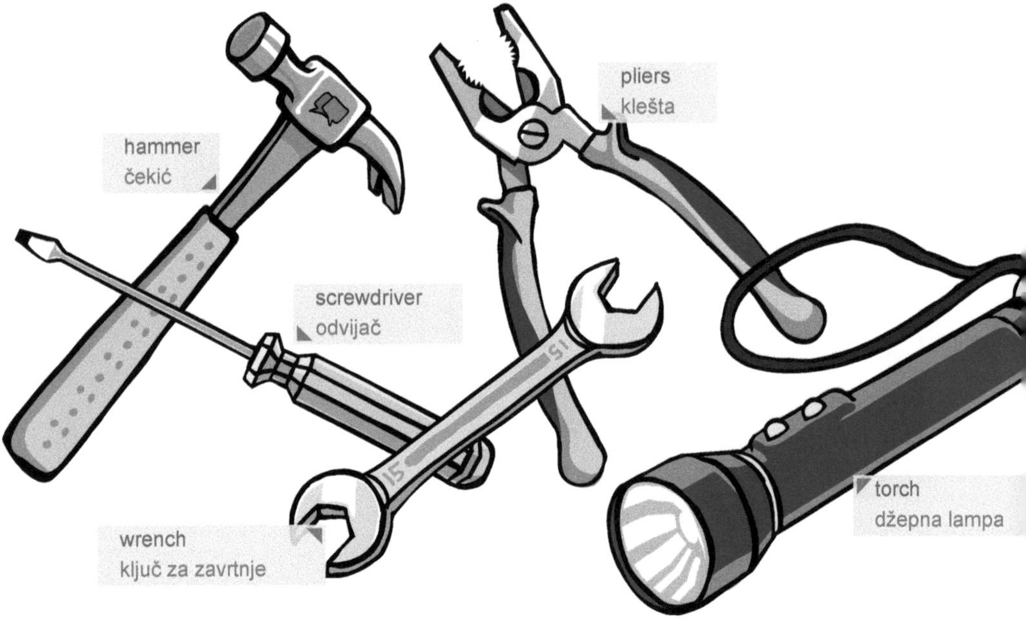

hammer
čekić
pliers
klešta
screwdriver
odvijač
wrench
ključ za zavrtnje
torch
džepna lampa

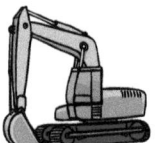

excavator

bager

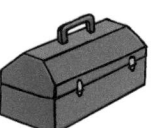

toolbox

kutija za alat

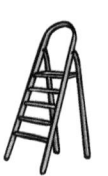

ladder

merdevine

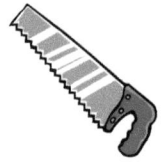

saw

pila

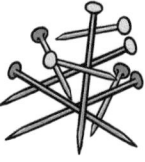

nails

ekser

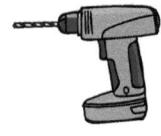

drill

bušilica

repair

popraviti

shovel

lopata

Damn!

do đavola!

dustpan

lopatica

paint can

lonac za boju

screws

zavrtanji

musical instruments
muzički instrument

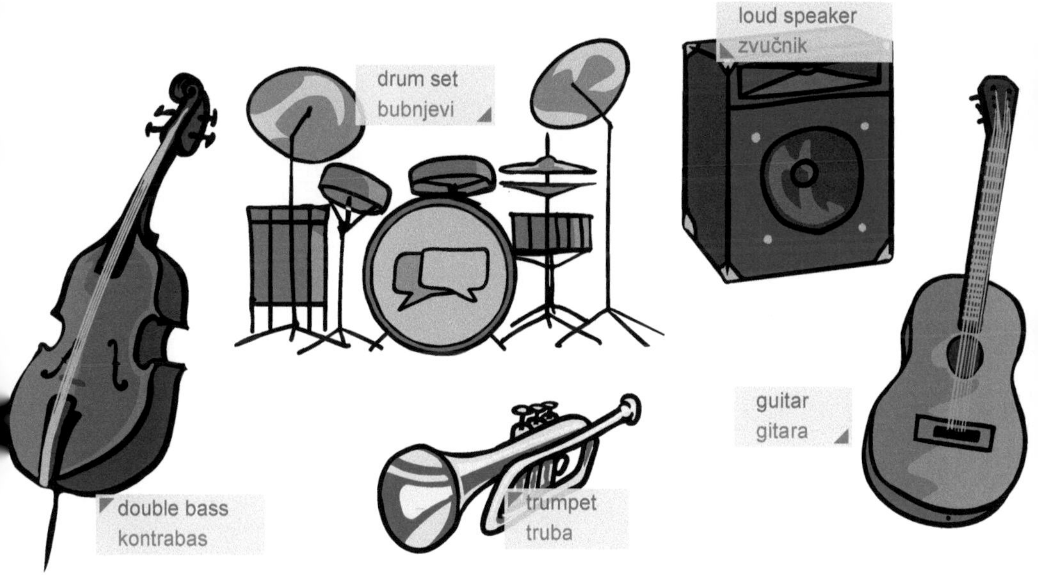

drum set
bubnjevi

loud speaker
zvučnik

guitar
gitara

double bass
kontrabas

trumpet
truba

piano

klavir

violin

violina

bass

bas

timpani

timpani

drums

udaraljke za bubnjeve

keyboard

tipke klavira

saxophone

saksofon

flute

flauta

microphone

mikrofon

zoo

zoološki vrt

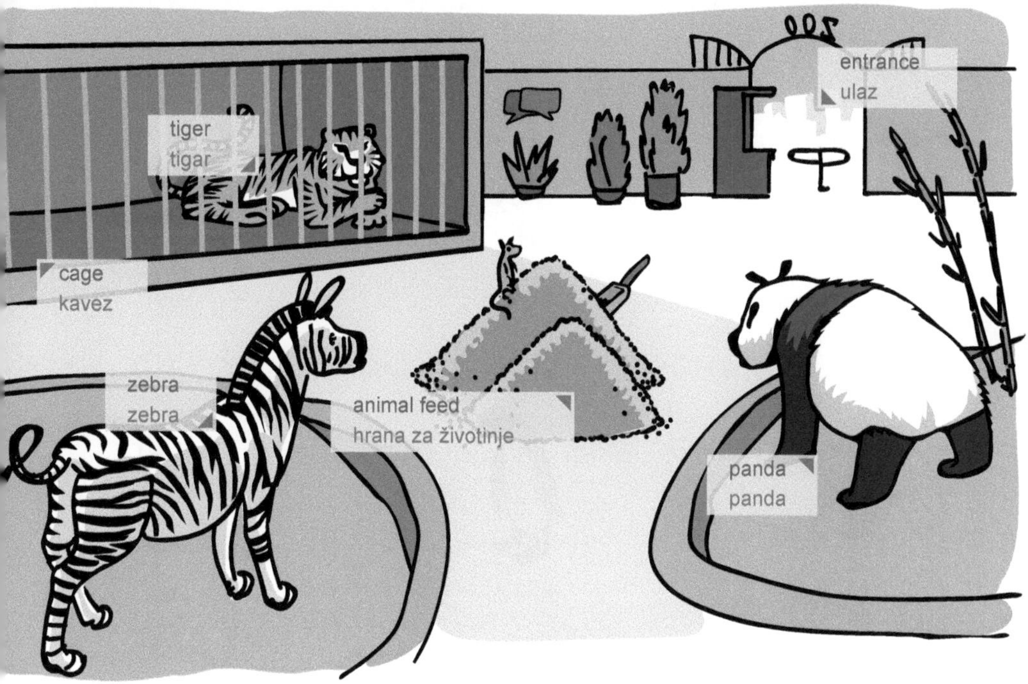

entrance
ulaz
tiger
tigar
cage
kavez
zebra
zebra
animal feed
hrana za životinje
panda
panda

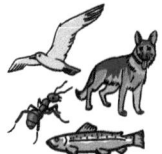

animals

životinje

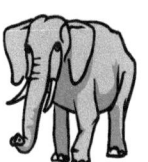

elephant

slon

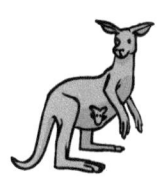

kangaroo

kengur

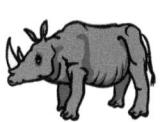

rhino

nosorog

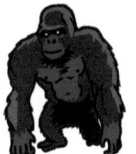

gorilla

gorila

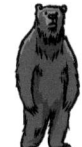

bear

medved

camel

kamila

ostrich

noj

lion

lav

monkey

majmun

flamingo

flamingo

parrot

papagaj

polar bear

polarni medved

penguin

pingvin

shark

ajkula

peacock

paun

snake

zmija

crocodile

krokodil

zookeeper

čuvar u zoološkom vrtu

seal

tuljan

jaguar

jaguar

pony

poni

leopard

leopard

hippo

nilski konj

giraffe

žirafa

eagle

orao

boar

divlja svinja

fish

riba

turtle

kornjača

walrus

morž

fox

lisica

gazelle

gazela

American football
američki nogomet

cycling
biciklizam

tennis
tenis

basketball
košarka

swimming
plivanje

boxing
boks

ice hockey
hokej na ledu

soccer

fudbal

badminton

badminton

athletics

atletika

handball

rukomet

skiing

skijanje

polo

polo

laugh
smejati se

jump
skočiti

hug
zagrliti

walk
ići

sing
pevati

dream
sanjati

pray
moliti se

kiss
poljubiti

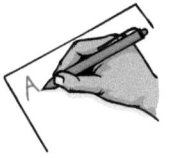

write

pisati

draw

crtati

show

pokazati

push

gurati

give

dati

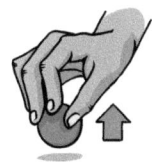

take

uzeti

have
imati

do
činiti

be
biti

stand
stojati

run
trčati

pull
povlačiti

throw
baciti

fall
padati

lie
ležati

wait
čekati

carry
nositi

sit
sediti

get dressed
oblačiti

sleep
spavati

wake up
probuditi se

look at

gledati

cry

plakati

stroke

milovati

comb

češljati

talk

govoriti

understand

razumeti

ask

pitati

listen

slušati

drink

piti

eat

jesti

tidy up

pospremiti

love

voleti

cook

kuhati

drive

voziti

fly

leteti

sail

ploviti

calculate

računati

read

čitati

learn

učiti

work

raditi

marry

venčati se

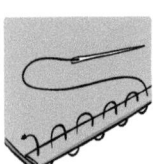

sew

šiti

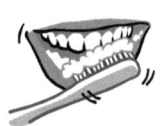

brush teeth

prati zube

kill

ubiti

smoke

pušiti

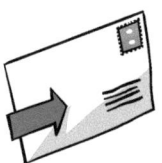

send

poslati

family
porodica

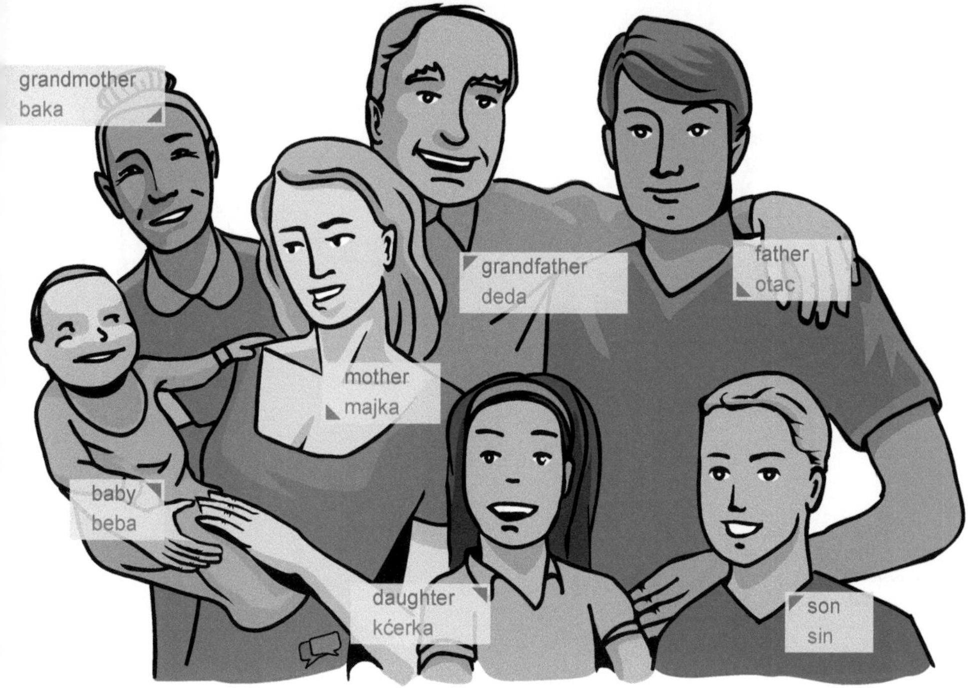
grandmother
baka
grandfather
deda
father
otac
mother
majka
baby
beba
daughter
kćerka
son
sin

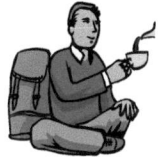

guest
gost

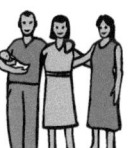

aunt
tetka

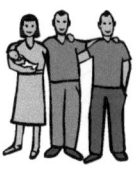

uncle
ujak, stric

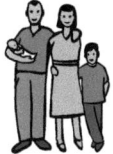

brother
brat

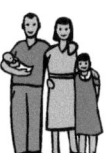

sister
sestra

body
telo

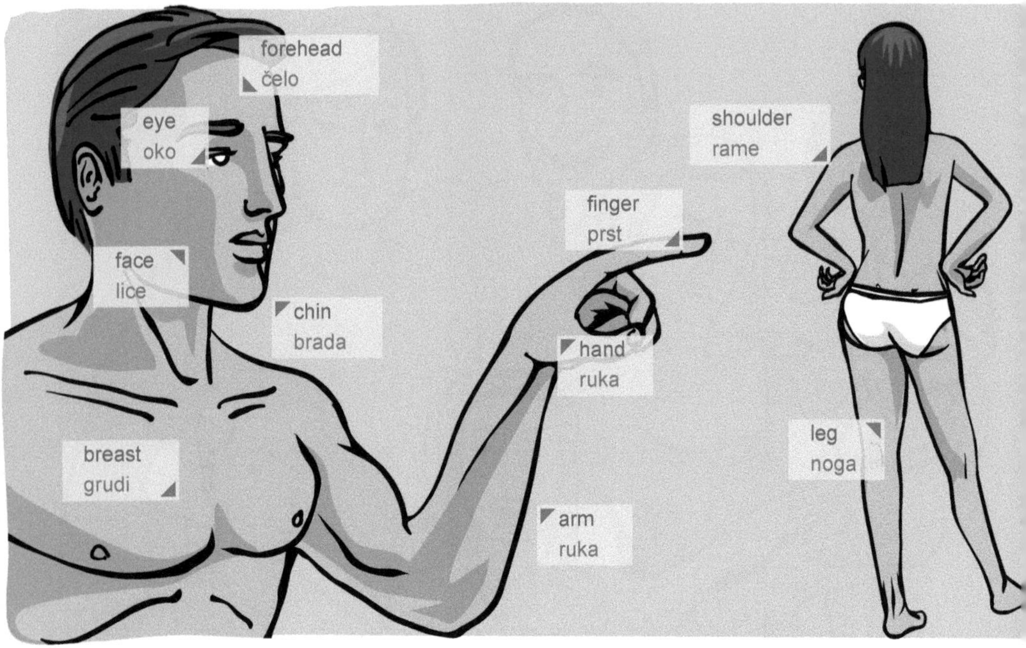

forehead
čelo

eye
oko

shoulder
rame

finger
prst

face
lice

chin
brada

hand
ruka

breast
grudi

leg
noga

arm
ruka

baby

beba

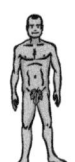

man

muškarac

woman

žena

girl

devojčica

boy

dečak

head

glava

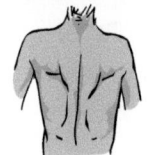

back

leđa

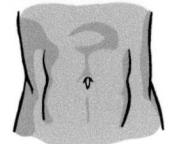

belly

stomak

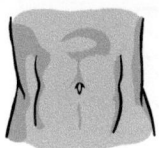

navel

pupak

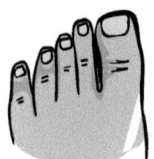

toe

nožni prst

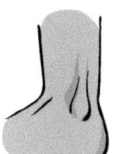

heel

peta

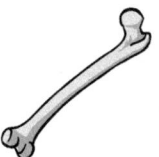

bone

kost

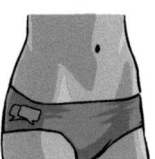

hip

kukovi

knee

koleno

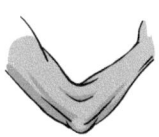

elbow

lakat

nose

nos

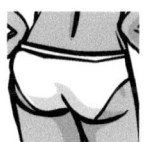

buttocks

zadnjica

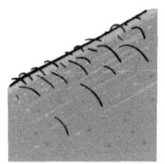

skin

koža

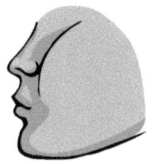

cheek

obraz

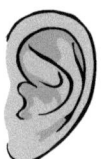

ear

uvo

lip

usna

mouth

usta

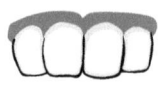

tooth

zub

tongue

jezik

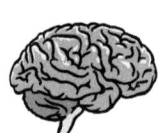

brain

mozak

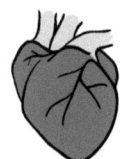

heart

srce

muscle

mišić

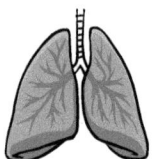

lung

pluća

liver

jetra

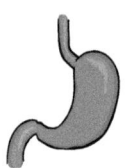

stomach

želudac

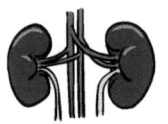

kidneys

bubrezi

sex

polni odnos

condom

kondom

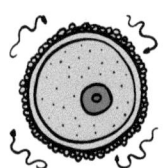

ovum

jajna ćelija

semen

sperma

pregnancy

trudnoća

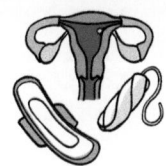

menstruation

menstruacija

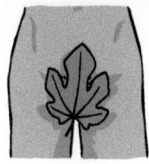

vagina

vagina

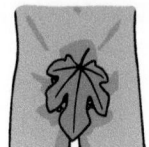

penis

penis

eyebrow

obrva

hair

kosa

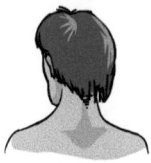

neck

vrat

hospital

bolnica

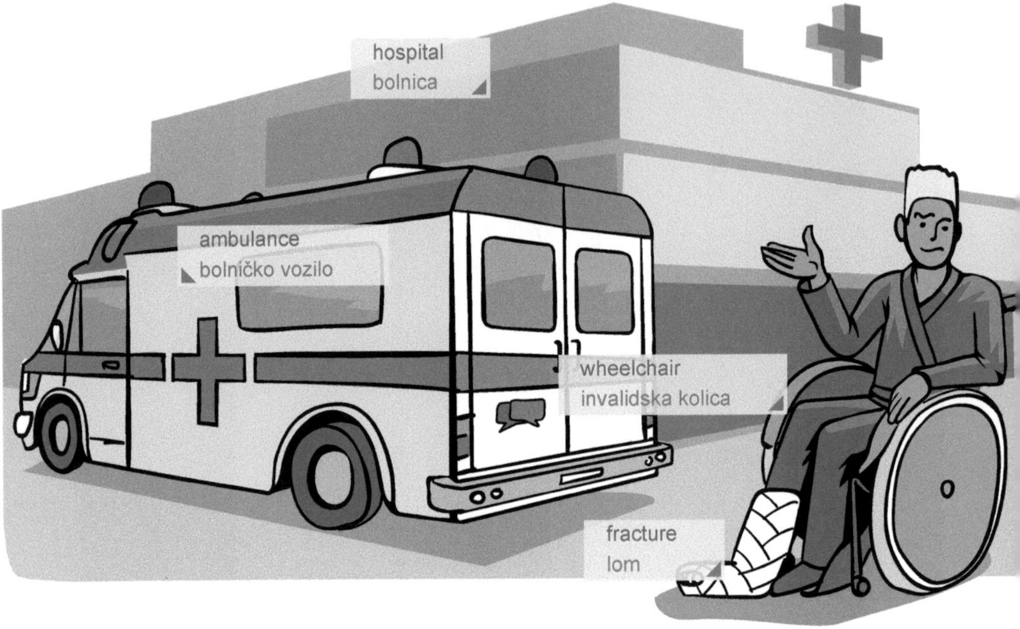

hospital
bolnica
ambulance
bolničko vozilo
wheelchair
invalidska kolica
fracture
lom

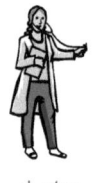

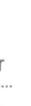

doctor

lekar

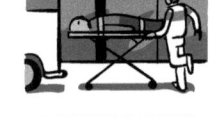

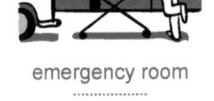

emergency room

hitna medicinska služba

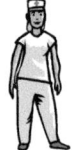

nurse

medicinska sestra

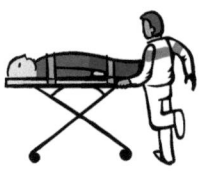

emergency

hitni slučaj

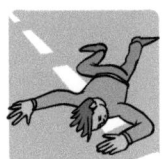

unconscious

nesvest

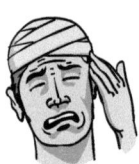

pain

bol

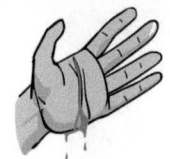

injury

povreda

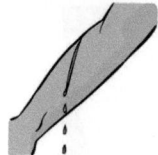

bleeding

krvarenje

heart attack

srčani udar

stroke

udar

allergy

alergija

cough

kašalj

fever

groznica

flu

gripa

diarrhea

proliv

headache

glavobolja

cancer

rak

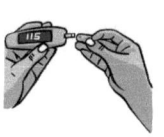

diabetes

dijabetes

surgeon

hirurg

scalpel

skalpel

operation

operacija

CT
ct

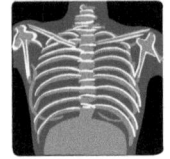

x-ray
rentgen

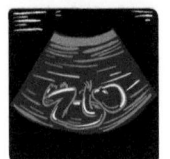

ultrasound
ultrazvuk

face mask
maska

disease
bolest

waiting room
čekaona

crutch
štaka

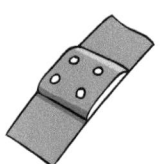

plaster
flaster

bandage
zavoj

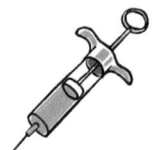

injection
injekcija

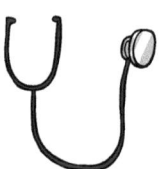

stethoscope
stetoskop

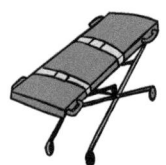

stretcher
nosila

clinical thermometer
termometar

birth
rođenje

overweight
prekomerna težina

hospital - bolnica

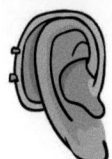

hearing aid
slušni aparat

disinfectant
sredstvo za dezinfekciju

infection
infekcija

virus
virus

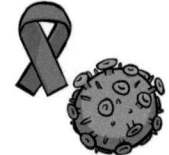

HIV / AIDS
HIV / AIDS

medicine
medicina

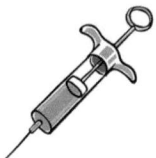

vaccination
vakcinacija

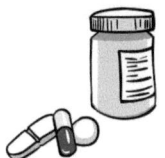

tablets
tablete

pill
pilula

emergency call
hitni poziv

blood pressure monitor
uređaj za merenje pritiska

ill / healthy
bolesno / zdravo

Help!	 alarm	 assault
pomoć!	alarm	nasrtaj

 attack	 danger	 emergency exit
napad	opasnost	izlaz u slučaju nužde

Fire!	 fire extinguisher	 accident
požar!	protivpožarni aparat	nezgoda

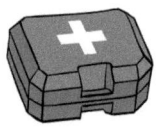 first-aid kit	 SOS	 police
kutija prve pomoći	sos	policija

Europe

Evropa

North America

Severna Amerika

South America

Južna Amerika

Africa

Afrika

Asia

Azija

Australia

Australija

Atlantic

Atlantik

Pacific

Pacifik

Indian Ocean

Indijski okean

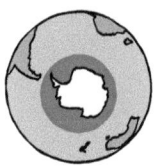

Antarctic Ocean

Antarktički okean

Arctic Ocean

Arktički ocean

North pole

Severni pol

South pole

Južni pol

Antarctica

Antarktik

earth

zemlja

land

zemlja

sea

more

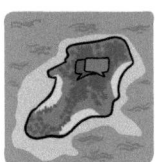

island

otok

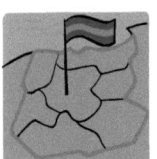

nation

nacija

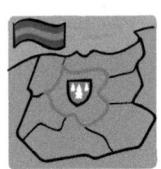

state

država

clock face

brojčanik sata

hour hand

satna kazaljka

minute hand

minutna kazaljka

second hand

sekundna kazaljka

What time is it?

Koliko je sati?

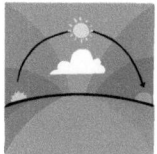

day

dan

time

vreme

now

sada

digital watch

digitalni sat

minute

minuta

hour

čas

week

sedmica

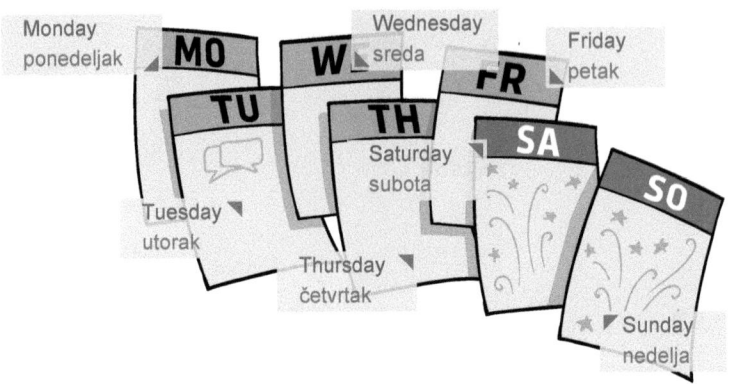

Monday / ponedeljak
Tuesday / utorak
Wednesday / sreda
Thursday / četvrtak
Friday / petak
Saturday / subota
Sunday / nedelja

yesterday
juče

today
danas

tomorrow
sutra

morning
jutro

noon
podne

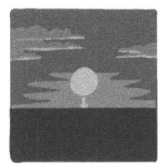

evening
veče

MO	TU	WE	TH	FR	SA	SU
1	2	3	4	5	6	7
8	9	10	11	12	13	14
15	16	17	18	19	20	21
22	23	24	25	26	27	28
29	30	31	1	2	3	4

workdays
radni dani

MO	TU	WE	TH	FR	SA	SU
1	2	3	4	5	6	7
8	9	10	11	12	13	14
15	16	17	18	19	20	21
22	23	24	25	26	27	28
29	30	31	1	2	3	4

weekend
vikend

| rain | | snow |
| kiša | | sneg |

| spring | wind |
| proleće | vetar |

| summer | fall |
| leto | jesen |

| | winter |
| | zima |

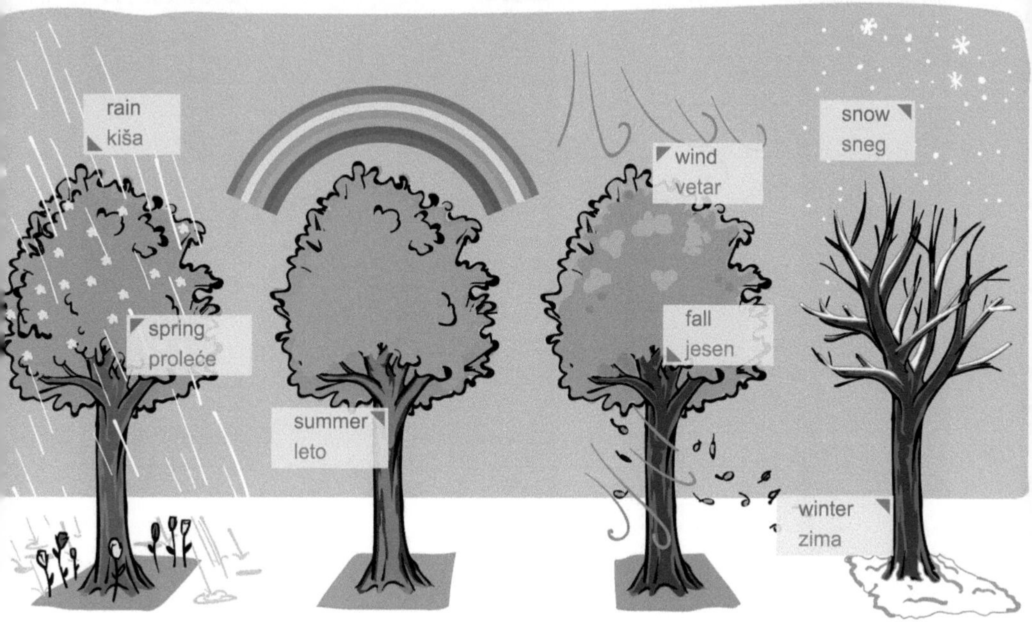

weather forecast

meteorološka prognoza

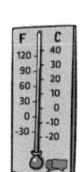

thermometer

termometar

sunshine

sunčana svetlost

cloud

oblak

fog

magla

humidity

vlažnost vazduha

lightning

munja

thunder

grmljavina

storm

oluja

hail

tuča

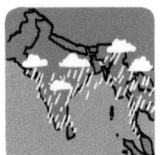

monsoon

monsun

flood

poplava

ice

led

January

januar

February

februar

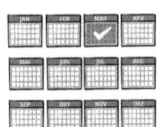

March

mart

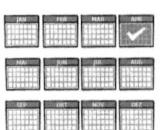

April

april

May

maj

June

juni

July

juli

August

avgust

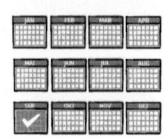

September
....
septembar

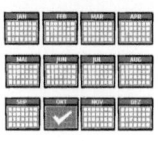

October
....
oktobar

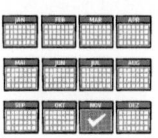

November
....
novembar

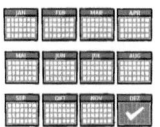

December
....
decembar

shapes
oblici

circle
....
krug

square
....
kvadrat

rectangle
....
pravougao

triangle
....
trougao

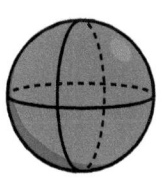

sphere
....
kugla

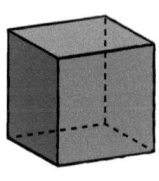

cube
....
kocka

white

bela

yellow

žuta

orange

narandžasta

pink

ružičasta

red

crvena

purple

ljubičasta

blue

plava

green

zelena

brown

smeđa

gray

siva

black

crna

a lot / a little
....
mnogo / malo

angry / calm
....
ljutito / mirno

beautiful / ugly
....
lepo / ružno

beginning / end
....
početak / kraj

big / small
....
veliko / maleno

bright / dark
....
svetlo / tamno

brother / sister
....
brat / sestra

clean / dirty
....
čisto / prljavo

complete / incomplete
....
potpuno / nepotpuno

day / night
....
dan / noć

dead / alive
....
mrtvo / živo

wide / narrow
....
široko / usko

edible / inedible

jestivo / nejestivo

evil / kind

zlo / dobro

excited / bored

uzbuđeno / dosadno

fat / thin

debelo / mršavo

first / last

na početku / na kraju

friend / enemy

prijatelj / neprijatelj

full / empty

puno / prazno

hard / soft

tvrdo / mekano

heavy / light

teško / lagano

hunger / thirst

glad / žeđ

ill / healthy

bolesno / zdravo

illegal / legal

ilegalno / legalno

intelligent / stupid

pametno / glupo

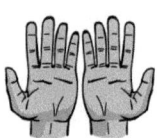

left / right

levo / desno

near / far

blizu / daleko

new / used

novo / polovno

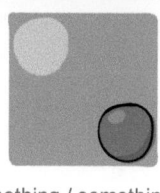

nothing / something

ništa / nešto

old / young

staro / mlado

on / off

uključeno / isključeno

open / closed

otvoreno / zatvoreno

quiet / loud

tiho / glasno

rich / poor

bogato / siromašno

right / wrong

tačno / pogrešno

rough / smooth

hrapavo / glatko

sad / happy

tužno / sretno

short / long

kratko / dugo

slow / fast

polako / brzo

wet / dry

mokro / suho

warm / cool

toplo / hladno

war / peace

rat / mir

0

zero

nula

1

one

jedan

2

two

dva

3

three

tri

4

four

četiri

5

five

pet

6

six

šest

7

seven

sedam

8

eight

osam

9

nine

devet

10

ten

deset

11

eleven

jedanaest

12

twelve

dvanaest

13

thirteen

trinaest

14

fourteen

četrnaest

15

fifteen

petnaest

16

sixteen

šestnaest

17

seventeen

sedamnaest

18

eighteen

osamnaest

19

nineteen

devetnaest

20

twenty

dvadeset

100

hundred

stotinu

1.000

thousand

hiljadu

1.000.000

million

milion

English
....
engleski

American English
....
američki engleski

Chinese Mandarin
....
mandarinski kineski

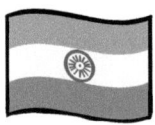

Hindi
....
hindski

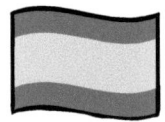

Spanish
....
španski

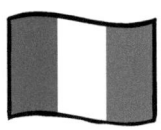

French
....
francuski

Arabic
....
arapski

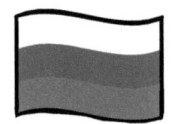

Russian
....
ruski

Portuguese
....
portugalski

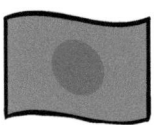

Bengali
....
bengalski

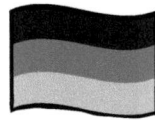

German
....
nemački

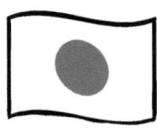

Japanese
....
japanski

I

ja

you

ti

he / she / it

on / ona / ono

we

mi

you

vi

they

oni

who?

Ko?

what?

Šta?

how?

Kako?

where?

Gde?

when?

Kada?

name

ime

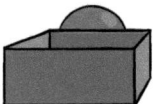

behind

iza

in

u

in front of

ispred

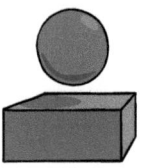

over

preko

on

na

under

ispod

beside

pored

between

između

place

mesto